NO AR

T5-AQQ-435

Everything You Need to Know About

DECISION-
MAKING

Although you make decisions every day, some, such as whether or not to take the cigarette your best friend offers you, are more difficult than others.

Everything You Need to Know About

DECISION-MAKING

Julie Parker

THE ROSEN PUBLISHING GROUP, INC.
NEW YORK

Published in 1996, 1998 by The Rosen Publishing Group, Inc.
29 East 21st Street, New York, NY 10010

Copyright © 1996, 1998 by The Rosen Publishing Group, Inc.

Revised edition 1998

Library of Congress Cataloging-in-Publication Data

Parker, Julie F.
    Everything you need to know about decision-making / Julie Parker.
Rev. ed.
    p. cm. — (The need to know library)
    Includes bibliographical references and index.
    Summary: Briefly discusses the process of decision-making,
emphasizing real situations in which teenagers may find themselves.
    ISBN 0-8239-2746-6
    1. Decision-making in adolescence—Juvenile literature.
[1. Decision-making.] I. Title. II. Series.
BF724.3.D47P37 1998
153.8'13—dc20

                                        92-39945
                                          CIP
                                          AC

Manufactured in the United States of America

Contents

1. Making Decisions   7

2. Taking Responsibility   13

3. Listening to Others   20

4. Listening to Yourself   31

5. Steps to Making Good Decisions   37

6. Making Mistakes   48

7. Making Choices for Success   56

    Glossary   59

    Where to Go for Help   61

    For Further Reading   62

    Index   63

Making your own decisions, such as how much money you can afford to withdraw and spend, is a large part of becoming an adult.

Chapter 1

Making Decisions

Making decisions is hard work. Even for adults, it is very difficult. Although adults often seem as if they have their lives in order, many do not make very smart decisions. Often, this happens because they never learned the skills of good decision-making.

You can encounter all sorts of problems when faced with a decision. You may not consider all the consequences of your choice. You may be blinded or led by your emotions and fail to think logically and clearly. You may choose your easiest option, even if it is not the best one. Or you may choose not to decide, allowing someone else to make your decision for you.

The ability to see situations clearly and to know what is best for you will help you throughout your life. Often you can avoid bad decisions if you think of all the different things that could happen as a result of your decision. You have to consider the consequences of your decision both for yourself and for others.

Would you cheat on a test? Would you deal drugs? Would you physically attack someone? Would you steal from someone?

Many people who make these mistakes find themselves in bad situations from which they do not know how to escape. Often their difficulties are the result of poor decisions they made in the past. If they had made better decisions, they might not be in such a bind today. They might not be in trouble or might not have broken the law.

You are already making many decisions for yourself, although you may not realize it. As you get older, however, your decisions become more complicated. Life can sometimes seem confusing and chaotic.

Seventeen-year-old Chuck is graduating from high school in a few months. He's not sure what he wants to do after that. It's not that he doesn't want to go to college; he just isn't interested in college very much, or in any kind of school for that matter.

His dad wants Chuck to be an engineer like him. His mom wants him to be a computer programmer, because the job brings a good salary. Chuck's friends want him to stay around the neighborhood and just hang out with them.

Chuck feels lost and confused. He thinks that if he stays around his old neighborhood, he will end up living at home forever. He knows that he can't get a job

Small decisions, such as what book to read, help prepare you for the big decisions you'll have to make in life, such as what career to choose.

that pays very well without a college education. But if he goes to college, he doesn't know what he would study there. Chuck has a lot of big decisions to make, but he doesn't know how, and he's running out of time.

Decisions, Decisions, Decisions

As a teenager, it may seem as though you have too many decisions to make. Some of these are small: what to wear to school, where to hang out with your friends, what to do this weekend. In addition to these choices, you also have to make decisions about your family, friends, education, job, dating, drugs, and many other things.

When you think about all these decisions at once, they may be overwhelming. However, they are often not as bad as they seem. If you practice some smart decision-making, you can think clearly of the best path to take in any situation.

It's Your Decision

The big decisions in your life are fairly easy to imagine. They may include things such as education, career, marriage, and children. Many people will have to make these big choices someday. Your smaller, daily decisions, however, are also important. They can have a big effect on your life in the long run. You should make these choices carefully, too.

When you have to make a decision, you can and probably should ask other people for their advice. However, you have to be able to see for yourself what

You can ask other people for their opinions on a decision you must make, but the final choice is up to you.

is good for you and what is not. This can be very difficult, and some people have trouble doing it. They cannot choose one option over another. They cannot stand up for themselves and for what they want. Instead, they try to say yes to everyone and to make everyone happy. An important part of decision-making is learning how to tell good advice from bad and how to say no to people.

Your teen years are a confusing time. The world may seen unfamiliar and even terrifying. However, with some guidance and decision-making tools, you can make smart decisions and succeed.

Allowing others to make decisions for you is called being passive.

Chapter 2

Taking Responsibility

If making decisions is so great, then how come so many people don't want to do it? Sometimes people are so afraid of making a mistake that they don't take responsibility for their decisions. Instead of thinking about a situation, they let their action (or lack of action) determine the outcome. Some of these habits of behavior can hurt themselves or others. Because of this, it can be good to recognize these patterns and see if you use them yourself.

Being Passive

How often have you heard someone ask, "What do you want?" and the other person says, "I don't care," or "I'm easy," or "Whatever"? The person who is not expressing his or her opinion is being *passive*. He or she does not want to make a decision and so pretends that it doesn't matter. This may seem like the easy way out, but really it is just the opposite.

Jorge is at the video store with his friends, Steve and Eduardo. They're hanging out tonight, and they decided to rent a movie and get a pizza.

"What do you want to see?" Steve asks. After look-ing around, Jorge picks out a few movies that he'd like. Eduardo and Steve are over in the horror section, looking at some really cheesy, gory movies. Jorge hates stuff like that. He thinks those movies are stupid. Plus, they always rent horror movies. He carries three videos over to his friends, but they look as though they've already decided on one.

"Why bother to show them what I want?" Jorge mutters to himself. "They never like what I like any-way." He shrugs and shoves the movies he chose back onto the shelf.

Jorge's big mistake here is being passive, which is unfair to everyone involved. He cheats himself because he doesn't like the movie and doesn't have a good time. Later on, if Jorge ends up regretting his decision, he may blame his friends—which would also be unfair.

While this example tells of just one small incident, many people are in the habit of being passive throughout their lives. Their decisions are made by whatever another person or group suggests. They may do this out of overeagerness to please someone else, even at their own expense. Perhaps they are so used to letting others decide that they don't take time to stop and consider, "Hey, what do *I* want here?" When it is time to make a decision, the passive person needs to stop and think seriously about what would be best for himself or herself, and then speak up.

Being Aggressive

The opposite of being passive is being *aggressive.* Aggressive people know what they want and go after it, but they think about themselves too much. The only people whose feelings they consider are themselves. They accomplish their goals at the expense of other people. Aggressive people may get what they want, but the physical and psychological cost to others can be high.

John is running for class president, and no one is going to stand in his way. He is planning to win at all costs. He has already strong-armed many of his classmates into voting for him. Now he is going after the other candidate, Caleb.

John and several of his friends walk slowly over to where Caleb is standing alone on the basketball court. While his friends look out for teachers, John slaps Caleb lightly in the face. He suggests that Caleb drop out of the race. "Otherwise," John says, "I'll be back to do more than just tap you."

John is not being fair. He is robbing Caleb of the chance to run for class office and the students of the opportunity to choose a president. Also, if Caleb tells a teacher what has happened, John may be forced to drop out of the election. One day he may try to intimidate the wrong person and end up in trouble. John's aggressive behavior is harmful to himself and to those around him.

Being Passive-Aggressive

Passive-aggressive behavior is saying one thing, but really meaning another. A passive-aggressive person pretends that whatever is decided doesn't matter to her or him (*passive*), while single-mindedly going after something (*aggressive*). Passive-aggressive people are dishonest with themselves. At the same time, they manipulate other people into doing what they want them to do.

Tiffany is leaving school late one afternoon, after a student government meeting. It's getting dark, and she's just thinking about that two-mile walk home, when Jeff, who is also in student government, bounds by her jingling his car keys.
"Hey Jeff, are you going home?" Tiffany calls to him.
"Sure. What's it look like?" Jeff answers.
"Well . . . um . . . where do you live?"
"Up near the elementary school . . . why?" Jeff asks.
"Oh, I'm way across town . . . I don't want to trouble you . . . I'll just walk the two miles myself . . .

Physically aggressive behavior is easier to spot than verbal or emotionally aggressive behavior.

it probably won't be totally *dark by the time I get home . . . chances are I'll be fine . . . hopefully,"* Tiffany says wistfully.*

Tiffany obviously wants a ride home but chooses not to come right out and ask for it. Her behavior is passive-aggressive, because she wants something and is going after it—while saying that it doesn't matter. She tries to make Jeff feel guilty for not driving her home without ever asking him if he would. Tiffany would make things a lot easier if she just decided to be forthright about what she wanted.

Being Assertive

Assertive people go after their objectives in a way that respects others and themselves. When you act assertively you state what you want honestly, while considering the feelings of others. You use "I" statements, describing your own thoughts and emotions, instead of blaming or second-guessing the other person.

Meredith's older sister, Amanda, has an eating disorder. Even though she is 5'4" and weighs 115 pounds, Amanda is convinced that she's fat. Recently Meredith has noticed Amanda going to the bathroom after dinner and locking the door for a long time. Meredith hears vomiting noises and knows that this eating disorder (bulimia) is serious and can be deadly. She wants her sister to stop, but doesn't know what to say to her.

***Passive approach**—Meredith worries about this but doesn't say anything.*

***Aggressive approach**—Meredith: "Amanda, I know that you are vomiting your dinner every night. I'm going to tell Mom and Dad and make them cut off your allowance until you stop it. I'll also go to the guidance couselor and she'll force you to get therapy or be suspended."*

***Passive-Aggressive**—"Amanda, I know you're ruining your life, but who cares? You want to starve to death—fine by me. Keep this up and before long you'll be like a skeleton. You want to look like that— swell—suit youself."*

***Assertive**—"Amanda, may I talk with you? I've heard you vomiting every night, and I'm really worried about you. I'm afraid that you are hurting yourself. Have you thought about getting some help? I care about you, and I'll do whatever I can to help."*

When you are assertive, you take responsibility for yourself and your own feelings. You know what you want to accomplish and then go for it in a way that respects others and yourself. Thinking and acting assertively are necessary for making and carrying out healthy decisions.

Chapter 3

Listening to Others

As you take responsibility for yourself, you learn how to consult with other people before making your own decision. When you need to decide something, do you ask other people for advice? Whether it's choosing an outfit for a party or a career for a lifetime, getting feedback from someone else can help you to make up your mind. Also hearing someone else's thoughts often puts things in perspective.

Good and Bad Advice

Since asking for advice is common, it is important to be able to tell the difference between good input and bad advice. Sometimes, even without realizing it, a friend may say something that is not in your best interest. You need to be able to decide what advice is helpful and what is best to ignore.

Jill and Mitchell have been going out for nine months. Now that it is summer, Mitchell's parents go away on the weekends; Mitchell has to stay home for his lifeguard job. He thinks that this would be the perfect time for him and Jill to have sex. He tells her that he loves her and that is all that matters. Jill likes Mitchell a lot—maybe she even loves him—but she is very confused about having sex. One Friday, she invites her two best friends, Veronica and Maureen, to sleep over. Late at night, when she's sure her parents are asleep, Jill asks them for their advice.

"Hey, you guys—promise you can keep a secret?" Jill begins.

"Yeah, sure, of course," Maureen and Veronica both answer. They know something juicy is coming up.

"Well . . . Mitchell wants to sleep with me . . . and I'm not sure what I should do."

"That's a secret?" asks Veronica. "Maybe to some people in Australia, but to those of us who know you it's pretty obvious what Mitchell wants. I think you should be fair to him—I mean, you've been going out for practically a year. Anyway, what's the big deal? Everyone's having sex."

"Not everyone," Maureen interrupts.

"Listen," continues Veronica, "do you want to be a virgin when you go off to college? Please. Now, as the expert here, let me tell you: Sex is not all it's cracked up to be, but I'm glad I've gotten it over with."

There are two kinds of advice: good advice and bad advice. Determine which you are being given before making a decision based on that advice.

Jill thinks for a second. "Perhaps I should just get it out of the way. I mean, Mitchell's a good guy, and sex has become this big thing between us. It probably wouldn't be so bad."

"Now wait a minute," says Maureen. "How do you feel about having sex with him?"

"Well . . . the idea is not unappealing . . ." Jill answers.

"If you said that about a restaurant we wouldn't go, and I think this is a little more important," Maureen observes. "Besides, have you thought about all the possible results of sex: sexually transmitted diseases, even AIDS, or a Jill-Mitchell kiddie?"

"How dramatic," says Veronica flatly.

"Hey, it could happen. Mitchell may not be a virgin—what about his sexual past? And no birth control is 100 percent foolproof—except for not having sex," Maureen counters. "Why don't you just wait until you know it's right for you, Jill? There's no rush."

"Maybe you're right," Jill answers. She seems relieved.

Both friends have advice for Jill—but which can help her and which might harm her? These checklists can help you tell the difference between good and bad advice.

Good Advice

- does not try to control
- causes you to think for yourself
- may steer you away from harmful options
- may provide additional information
- leaves you feeling at ease and resolved with your decision.

Bad Advice

- tries to dominate (control)
- may serve the other person's self-interest
- may lead you to harmful situations

- may withhold information
- leaves you feeling unsure and conflicted about the decision you've made
- causes you to rationalize and look for reasons why this decision would be okay.

Which friend is thinking more of Jill here—and which one is thinking of herself? Veronica tries to make up Jill's mind for her, saying that she owes sex to Mitchell. Since Veronica has already had sex and obviously doesn't feel that great about her experience, maybe she wants Jill to understand what she's been through. Veronica also doesn't tell Jill that she's sorry she had sex. Veronica had heard that sex is supposed to be wonderful, and when she remembers losing her virginity she just feels miserable. She does not think about the risks you run when you have sex, nor does she suggest that Jill think about them. When Jill first agrees to sleep with Mitchell, she makes up reasons for telling herself that this is right. This is called *rationalizing* and is a warning sign that the decision may be wrong. Also Veronica's line that "Everybody's doing it" simply is not true. Whatever "it" may be, there are always some people who think for themselves.

That is what Maureen helps Jill to do. Maureen asks Jill how she feels and points out that Jill should listen to her own mixed emotions. Maureen reminds Jill of some of the possible dangers of having sex. When Jill decides that she does not need to have sex to please someone else but should think of what she wants for herself first, she feels as if a weight has been taken off her shoulders. Feeling comfortable with a decision is usually a sign that it is right.

Where to Go for Advice

Even without realizing it, you are getting advice from lots of sources that tell you what you should do. Advertisers spend billions of dollars each year to influence your decisions about what you will eat, drink, wear, drive, and own. Famous models and sports figures urge you to purchase certain products. Since these companies and celebrities try to persuade you to spend money that goes to them, they are not reliable sources of influence. A good source of advice respects your ability to make your own decisions. Which of these sources may be the most helpful for you?

Peers (Friends Your Age)

The first place teenagers usually turn for advice is their friends. Because of this, it is important to choose your friends carefully. True friends will take the time to listen to you and show they care by their interest, support, and loyalty.

Sometimes your friends may want you to be like

Teenagers often try their first drink or drug with their friends as a result of negative peer pressure.

them, even if it means doing something harmful. The unspoken message that you should be like everyone else is called *peer pressure*. Although peer pressure is usually associated with doing something that hurts you, there is both good and bad peer pressure. For example, the pressure to smoke with friends would be bad peer pressure because smoking is an addictive habit that causes heart and lung diseases, as well as being expensive and smelly. On the other hand, the pressure to study and do well in school would be good peer pressure because it would create better possibilities for you after graduation and help you make the most of yourself.

Family

Whether or not you feel you can turn to a member of your family depends on your relationship with them. Does your mother or father take the time to listen to you, especially when you are upset? Do you have a brother or sister who understands you well? Maybe you have a relative with good judgment. Since your family members have known you from a very young age, they might understand what decision would be best for you.

Teachers and Guidance Counselors

Are there adults at your school who seem to know what to do? Sometimes students ask a teacher whom they respect for her or his opinion. Your guidance counselor is professionally trained to help you make decisions about academic options, such as where to apply for college, and find resources for personal problems like where to go for help for a drug or alcohol problem. Trust your gut feeling about people; if they seem trustworthy and wise, you might ask for their input or draw upon their expertise.

Books and Libraries

If you need factual or background information before making a decision, your school or public library can help. Suppose you are considering a career field like computer programming. Your library probably has books on this subject that are specifically focused on career exploration. The librarian could work with you to find the resources you need.

Authorities on a Given Subject

Suppose you are about to buy your first car. You can't afford a new one, and you don't want to throw away the money you've saved on a lemon. Here it would be important to consult with someone who knows cars well, like a mechanic, before deciding whether or not to buy a certain car. Professionals who offer their advice may charge for their services, but the investment is usually worth it.

Counselors and Clergy

Social workers, therapists, guidance counselors, psychologists, ministers, rabbis, and priests have all been professionally trained to listen well. They can help you ask the right questions of yourself as you work toward finding answers.

People whom you trust can help you reach your own good decisions.

You might talk to an old friend or someone else you trust for advice on a decision you must make.

Sometimes it helps to write down your feelings about a decision you need to make.

Chapter 4

Listening to Yourself

Voices Inside You

Even before you ask someone else for advice, you are getting the opinions of other people. You (and everyone else) carry around voices inside you from memories of what you have been taught when you were young. These thoughts influence how you feel about yourself and, as a result, how you act. For example, you may have been told to "Act like a lady," meaning that you should be sweet and accepting, or to "Act like a man," meaning that you should be tough and unemotional, no matter how you are feeling. Perhaps you were instructed, "If you can't say anything nice, don't say anything at all," or "Only sissies cry." These voices tell you what you "should" do, on the basis of someone else's notion of proper behavior. When you recognize how these thoughts and memories influence you,

you can think more clearly when making a decision.

Being Your Own Friend

When you hear these voices in your mind, try to notice if they are helpful or hurtful. Are they voices that encourage you and place things in perspective, or are they ready to put you down and beat you up for a simple mistake? Respond to the voices that are on your side.

Chris is deciding if he should go to the prom or not. On one hand, he thinks that it might be fun, and some of his friends are going. On the other hand, it is an expensive night, he's not sure whom he would ask to go with him, and a few of the guys he hangs out with are putting down the whole idea of going to this big dance. He finds himself thinking about this a lot as the dance gets closer, and he says to himself:

"I'd probably have a lousy time, because not all my friends will be there. Who would want to go with me anyway? I probably couldn't get a date. It's such a hassle renting a tuxedo and figuring out all the arrangements. What a waste of money. Besides, I'm not a good dancer; people might make fun of me."

Chris is being his own enemy here; the voices inside him are not giving him a chance to try something he might enjoy. But when Ann, a girl Chris likes, asks him to the prom, he realizes that he does want to go. The voices inside him begin to sound different.

"The prom is a once-in-a-lifetime experience, and it should be fun. Sure it costs money, but I've saved up enough to pay for my ticket, and Ann will pay for hers. I know enough people who will be there—we'll all sit together and have a good time. I can dance well enough; besides, you don't have to dance all night."

Here Chris is sounding like a friend to himself, since this voice is encouraging and supportive. Now he feels happy and eager when he thinks about going to the prom. The voices inside his head change, and his emotions also tell him that this decision is right.

Listening to Your Feelings

When you take the time to listen to yourself, your own emotions are a big help in figuring out whether a decision is right or not. Do you feel excited and energized by one option? Does another make you sigh with resignation? Does one possibility make you worried or nervous about what could happen as a result? Does a certain decision suddenly make you feel at ease? Listen to those feelings.

It's Matthew's first week in his new school, and he wants to make a good impression. He hasn't made too many friends yet, so when Bob, a guy in his math class, invites him to a party on Saturday night, he can hardly wait. "I may not know many people here, but if I show up at the party, they'll think I'm pretty cool," Matt figures.

On Saturday, when Matt gets to the party, he knows right away that this isn't like other parties he's attended. No lights are on, no parents are in sight, and everyone's smoking pot. Matt doesn't know anyone. He starts to feel uncomfortable, but Bob appears next to him. Matt is slightly relieved.

"My man Maaatty!" Bob yells over the stereo. "What's up?" Matt feels really uncomfortable now. Bob is weaving back and forth and slurring his words. Hazy masses of what look like people fill the corners of the room. Bob extends his hand to Matt. "Crunch all you want. I've got more," he says. Bob puts a little blue pill in Matt's hand and sways off into the next room.

Now Matt is really confused. His stomach is tied in knots. "If I want everyone to think that I'm cool, I should take this," he tells himself. "Then again, what is it, and who are all these people anyway?" he wonders. Just then, Bob comes back. "Hey, Maaatty! You having a good time or what?"

Matt doesn't know why he is here. Everyone seems so weird, including Bob. He wonders if he really wants to be friends with these people. A little voice inside him is saying that he probably doesn't.

Matt excuses himself, goes into the bathroom, and rinses the pill down the drain. When he comes out, he heads toward the kitchen, looking for a phone to call his parents for a ride. After talking briefly to his Dad, Matt makes his way to the front door to wait for his parents outside.

Matthew was uncomfortable. His feelings told him that this was a dangerous place that could cause him to mess up his body and his mind. Instead of going along with what the people around him were doing, Matthew decided to leave a potentially harmful situation. He listened to his own emotions.

Matthew also listened to his conscience. His parents and teachers had taught him that taking drugs is scary and stupid. An inner voice told Matthew clearly that this was the wrong thing to do.

Listening to Your Body

Your body also gives you clues about what is right for you. Just as Matthew felt a knot in the pit of his stomach when he was offered drugs, physical reactions like sweaty palms, tense muscles, a dry mouth, rapid heartbeat, or perspiration are your body's way of telling you something. Maybe a decision is causing you joyful excitement and so your heart is pounding.

Or perhaps you're thinking about your chemistry exam tomorrow. It's your worst subject, and you're not prepared. You may feel dread, and your legs may turn to jelly. You're terribly tense and can't stop sweating.

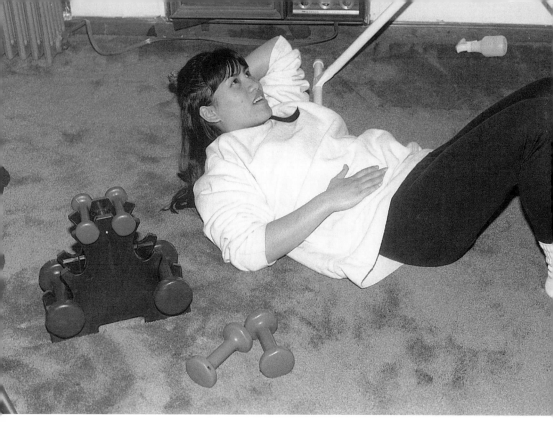

Exercise is one way you might choose to deal with your body's reaction to a decision in your life.

Either way, your body is letting you know that this decision is powerful.

What Do You Want?

You are the best expert on yourself, and you know how a certain choice will or won't work for you. Some people listen to themselves by writing in a journal or diary. Others go on walks or jogs so they can sort out possibilities in their mind. When making a decision, remember that your own opinion is the most important.

Chapter 5

Steps to Making Good Decisions

When you need to make a big decision, do you agonize over the possibilities in your mind? This may leave you feeling more confused. However, if you had to figure out a math problem, you would probably take out pencil and paper and follow the steps needed to solve it. Sometimes making a decision is also easier when you have a process to follow. Here are some steps that might help you address situations head-on.

1. Ask yourself, "What's my main goal?"

Allison can't decide if she should get a job after school. Her friend Jennifer works in a clothing store where there is an open position that Allison could probably get. Allison feels torn. She earns some money baby-sitting but thinks it would be great to have extra income for clothes and going out with her friends. But if she has to be at the store a few afternoons a week, she won't be able to try out for a lead in the school play. She is unsure what to do until she asks herself, "What do I want for myself in the long run?" Then she realizes that what is most important to her is getting into a good college. Being involved in extracurricular activities and having more time to study would help her college applications more than working at a store. Allison decides to not to apply for the job, even though it would have been fun to have the money.

By asking herself, "What do I want to achieve?" Allison has made a decision that helps her accomplish her goals by thinking about what really matters to her. Sometimes simply looking at where you want to go leads you to decisions that take you there.

2. Explore all the options

Tony's friends are planning to go to the movies together on Sunday afternoon. Tony would like to go, but he's not sure if he can afford it. Ever since his parents got divorced money has been tight, and Tony uses the money he earns from odd jobs to pay for his own clothes. He feels too embarrassed to admit this to his friends and decides to make up an excuse and just stay home. His mother notices that

Budgeting your money involves determining your priorities before deciding how and where to spend your money.

he seems a bit glum and asks him what is the matter. When Tony tells her, his mother suggests that he and his friends might find something else to do. She suggests that they play football or come over to the house to watch a game on television. It would be a cheaper afternoon, and they could still have a good time together.

Sometimes there are solutions that might not be obvious at first. If you can't figure out what to do, complete this sentence: "In the best of all possible worlds . . .". Tony thought that he could either go out with his friends or stay home by himself. But

ideally, Tony can find a way to have a good time
with his friends without spending a lot. They
might play a game or catch some sports on
television. If his friends still wanted to go out,
Tony might meet up with them after the movie. He
could budget a certain amount of money for his
time with them and be careful not to spend any
more. He might also decide not to buy any more
new clothes for a while and use the money from
his jobs for going out with friends in the future.
Often there are more options than the ones
presented; you just need to be creative and find
them.

3. Gather information and other helpful input

*Kathryn is in shock. Her period was three weeks
late, and so she bought a home pregnancy test. Her
fears were realized when she discovered that she was
pregnant. She and her boyfriend Darroll had been
sleeping together for six months. They always used a
condom, but one time it broke. Kathryn can't believe
her bad luck and doesn't know what to do. But she
knows that she needs to decide soon.*

*She tells Darroll that she is pregnant, and he
swears that he'll stand by her no matter what
happens. He says he'll even marry her if she wants.
But Kathryn does not want to get married at age
seventeen. She looks in the phone book and calls her*

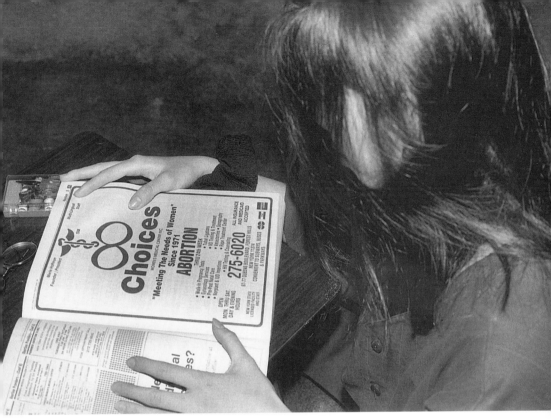

In order to make the decision that is right for you, you must weigh your options carefully, and consider all the possible consequences of your final choice.

local Planned Parenthood center, which arranges for her to meet with a counselor. Next Kathryn goes to the library and reads about teen pregnancy. In a book she discovers an organization in Washington, D.C., called the National Committee for Adoption. She gets their number from directory assistance and calls them; they then send her information on adoption alternatives. After reading the literature they sent, she doesn't feel that she could give up the baby once it was born.

    Kathryn had never thought of herself as very religious, but now she is praying a lot. After a few days of soul-searching, she decides to tell her mother *what has happened. At first her mother is mad, but then she feels upset and worried about Kathryn's future. Kathryn is too. She knows one acquaintance from school who dropped out the year before to have a baby and is now living on welfare. Kathryn knows that abortion is safe and legal, and she does not feel that the embryo inside her is a life yet. She decides to end her pregnancy.*

Kathryn uses information and others' opinions to help her reach this difficult decision. Darroll says he will stay by her if she has the baby, and her mother is concerned about what having a baby would do to Kathryn. She reads about teen pregnancy in books and goes over the information from Planned Parenthood and the National Committee for Adoption. She thinks long and hard about what to do, and knows that ultimately the decision is hers. Kathryn does not believe that having an abortion is morally wrong, and so she chooses this option in good conscience.

4. List the arguments for and against (pro and con) a certain choice

Before she goes through with the abortion, Kathryn starts having doubts. She wonders what the operation will be like and stays awake one night worrying about this. Since she can't sleep and feels tormented, Kathryn turns on the light, goes to her desk, and takes out pencil and paper. She makes two columns to write down her thoughts so she can think more clearly about this important decision.

HAVING A BABY

Pro	**Con**
• *bring life into this world*	• *not ready to be a mother now*
• *babies are fun and cute*	• *babies require a lot of work*
• *have baby and give it up for adoption*	• *unsure if I could give up baby*
• *have baby and marry Darroll (?)*	• *too young to get married*
	• *going to high school while pregnant, worse dropping out*
	• *pain of giving birth*
	• *no job skills to support self and baby*
	• *going to college is very difficult*
	• *having a good career is very difficult*

Once Kathryn has written down her reasons, she feels comforted. Seeing the list in front of her helps her to understand what caused her to make this choice. She knows that this is the right decision for her at this time.

5. Ask yourself if this decision hurts you or someone else

Jed is nervous because he has to take the Scholastic Aptitude Test (SAT) for college entry in five days. He has studied for weeks, but he has a problem freezing up on tests. He is sitting in the cafeteria during lunch talking about the test with some friends when a guy he knows, Michael, pipes up.

"Jed, no need to be so nervous," Michael begins.

"That's easy for you to say, but I have a hard time taking tests . . ." Jed explains.

"Listen," Michael continues, "I'll lend you my friend." With a wink, Michael reaches into his backpack and pulls out a small pocket dictionary. "Just use this for the verbal section. The gym where you take the test is so huge, and all those proctors do is sit at their desks anyway. I'm sure that this paper pal brought my score up 100 points."

Since his friends are looking at him, Jed takes the dictionary.

"Uh . . . thanks, Michael," Jed says.

But as the day of the test draws near, Jed isn't sure what to do. Would it be right to use a dictionary when this is clearly cheating? On the other hand, Jed feels that if no one finds out, what harm is done? Besides, no one is really hurt by it, and the difference just might help him get into his top choice of schools.

Jed needs to decide if using a dictionary is the right (moral) or wrong (immoral) action to take. Since he finds himself rationalizing, he is probably on the wrong track. While it may not be obvious, cheating on the exam does hurt people. First, Jed hurts himself. If he already gets nervous on tests, the added stress of worrying about being caught with a dictionary could cause him to think less clearly. Cheating would also be unfair to the other students who studied for the exam and took it honestly. A decision that hurts you or others is wrong and should be avoided.

6. Think through the consequences or results of your decision

As Jed is debating about what to do, he pictures what might happen if he used the dictionary during the test. First he envisions himself going into the exam room very calm and collected. He imagines taking the test, sneaking peeks at the dictionary, then later getting a great score. When he sees how well he did, Jed figures that he'll be so happy about it he'll just forget about the cheating and not feel bad at all. That's one possible scenario.

On the other hand, Jed thinks about the possible negative consequences of cheating. He imagines getting a good test score but feeling miserable about knowing that it really doesn't belong to him. Worse, he wonders about getting caught. Suppose the proctor sees him cheating and takes the dictionary from him in front of everyone. He would be forced to leave the test and would be reported to school officials. This would seriously hurt his chances of getting into a good college. On top of all that, Jed knows that the word would travel around the school about what had happened. He thinks about how horribly embarrassed he would feel in front of his friends and teachers.

Before making a decision, you need to think through what might happen as a result. Ask yourself how you might benefit or lose from different outcomes. Also consider how your decision would affect anyone else involved in the situation. Once you weigh the consequences, the right decision may be more obvious.

7. Take time to make your decision

As the test date approaches, Jed is still undecided. Michael keeps on telling him what a breeze the exam will be with the dictionary. So Jed decides to "try on" each decision for a day to see how they feel. On the Thursday before the test he thinks that he will take the dictionary in with him. He notices that he feels worried and his stomach knots up. He feels uncomfortable talking with friends about the exam, as if he already had something to hide. On Friday, he thinks that he will not take the dictionary in with him. This time, Jed is a little more relaxed. He doesn't worry about getting caught cheating; he just thinks about getting in the room and giving the exam his best shot. He decides that this decision feels better, and so he follows his own instinct and takes the test honestly.

Here Jed has some time to make his decision, and he uses it well. There are times, however, when you need to decide something immediately. If you need to make a decision right away (such as what to put on for school that day), you might whiz the possibilities through your mind quickly. At times, though, someone might pressure you to make a decision before you need to or are ready. If someone keeps pressuring you, it is best either to let him know when you will give him an answer or just to refuse.

8. Make your decision

By following this process, you will have a way to address decisions you need to make. You can develop positive thinking habits, just as you might have good habits for taking care of your appearance or improving your mind. When you take solid steps to make your decisions, you can proceed with confidence.

Chapter 6

Making Mistakes

Whenever you make a decision, you run the risk of making a mistake. Perhaps you decide something that gets you in trouble. Maybe you end up feeling embarrassed or ashamed. A bad decision is one that hurts you or someone else. When you need to choose between possibilities, it is good to ask yourself if the result could be harmful to anyone. If so, that decision should be avoided.

But sometimes you might make a decision with good intentions, only to discover that things didn't work out the way you planned. You regret what you have done and feel miserable. When that happens, it is best to confront the mistake head-on. By dealing with the problem honestly, you avoid further complications later. Also, admitting that you have done something wrong usually earns respect. You feel better about your own ability, instead of feeling guilty or full of self-pity. Ask yourself, "What can I do to make the best of this situation?" When you try to learn from what has happened, even making a poor decision can help you in the future.

How Much Does This Matter?

When a decision you make does not turn out well, first ask yourself, "How much does this matter?" Without perspective, you might stay mad at yourself for a mistake that is not very serious. Don't blow a small issue way out of proportion. If the problem is small, just fix it and go on. Recognizing that a problem exists can help you correct it so that the situation doesn't become worse.

Carolina and her friends have decided to hang out together and rent a movie for the night. Since everyone is coming over to Carolina's house, she went to get the movie.

That night Elizabeth, Rosa, and Marisol gather at Carolina's house. The popcorn is popped, the soda is poured, and they are all looking forward to a fun film. But the movie stinks. After just a few minutes, they start to get bored. Carolina sees that her friends aren't having a good time, and she feels lousy because she selected this movie. Elizabeth murmurs, "Great movie, Carolina. NOT." Carolina hears this but pretends she doesn't. "Oh great, I should have

You may fear displeasing someone such as a boyfriend or girlfriend with a decision you make. This fear is common, but try not to let it stop you from deciding what's best for you.

gotten something else," she thinks. Carolina continues to feel awful. She starts listing in her mind all the other movies that the video store had that would have been better. She gets mad at herself for ruining what should have been a good time. Over and over she tells herself that no one is having fun. Without anyone's realizing it, Carolina makes sure that she feels the worst of anyone.

Then she stops herself. "This isn't such a big deal," she remembers. She walks over to the VCR and puts it on pause. "Okay, you guys," she announces, standing in front of the TV, "anyone care to see the end of this? . . . Do you want to go get another movie? It's not too late. Or do you want to just hang out and forget about watching a movie altogether?"

Then Elizabeth pipes up, "What's on TV?"

"Take a look," Carolina says, handing her the weekly television schedule.

"I'm tired of watching anyway," adds Rosa. "Why don't we just play Pictionary?"

"Yeah, that's a good idea," Marisol chimes in. "Carolina and I will team up against you two. How about it?"

Within minutes the girls are laughing at their silly drawings and having a great time. Recognizing that she had made a decision that disappointed everyone and then doing something about it, Carolina was able to do what she set out to do: have a fun night with her friends.

You may not realize until much later that a decision you have made, such as drinking alcohol with friends, was wrong. It is best to admit the mistake and learn from it.

Bigger Mistakes

Some mistakes that you make are more serious because the consequences that result from what you said or did can be very harmful. Because you run the risk of getting in big trouble, you probably hope that you don't get caught and later may want to pretend that the situation did not happen at all. It is also very tempting to try to shift the blame onto someone else. However, bigger mistakes usually lead to deeper investigation. If you have made a mistake, you are more honest with yourself and others if you own up to what you've done, correct it in any way you can, and make sure that you don't do it again.

"Hey, Kev, thanks for a great time," Louis calls to his buddy, Kevin, as he leaves the party.

"You, homeboy, are a party animal," Kevin jokes, putting his arm around Louis's shoulder. "You really did your fair share in knocking off those kegs of beer. You need some help getting home?"

"Me? Nah, I feel great, never felt better, yup, I am a-okay," Louis shouts over the music. He weaves his way to his parents' car, looking unsteady on his feet. When he gets behind the wheel he vaguely recalls being told not to drink and drive.

"I'm not that drunk," Louis thinks.

On his way home, Louis doesn't notice a red light. Another car screeches to a halt and just barely misses him. The driver pulls over and screams at Louis. Louis tells himself what an idiot the other driver is and keeps on going. When he gets home, Louis tries to pull his car into the driveway, but he misses. Instead he drives into the "SLOW—Children at Play" sign in front of his house. The front bumper gets banged in and the sign doubles over on itself. Louis starts to realize that he has been driving drunk. He feels awful about the car and relieved that his parents did not wake up at the sound of the crash. In the morning he will have to decide what to tell them, but for now all he wants to do is sleep.

When Louis wakes up, his parents are downstairs

having breakfast. He wonders what he should tell them. On one hand, he could make up a lie that the neighbor's cat ran in front of the car while he was pulling into the driveway, so he swerved to avoid hitting it and crashed into the sign. Or he could tell them the truth. Not admitting that he drove drunk feels easier, but Louis also knows that it may catch up with him. His lie doesn't make much sense because if he had seen the cat he could have just stopped the car, so his parents may not believe him. Also, Louis wonders if that other driver took down his license plate number and will report him. Louis decides that it is better to come clean now than have to keep worrying about what might happen if his parents found out later. He will tell them what he did wrong and let them know how sorry he is. Maybe he should to offer to pay for the damage to the car, even though he knows that won't be cheap. Louis knows that a car with a drunk driver becomes a death machine, and he decides never to repeat such a stupid mistake. With this resolved, he goes downstairs to face his parents.

By admitting that he has made this mistake, Louis is showing maturity that should gain him some respect. Of course, his parents won't be happy when they learn what he has done, but they may appreciate his honesty. Louis may have to suffer some consequences, like not being able to drive his parents' car for a while, but at least he doesn't have to keep carrying this around on his conscience. By admitting his mistake, making amends for it, and promising not to repeat it, Louis has the chance to start again.

When you face your mistakes head-on, you keep problems from getting bigger. It may take a lot of strength and conviction to change a situation, but often you will gain the respect of others—and yourself. Difficult decisions can become learning situations. Remember that everyone makes mistakes—it's what you do afterward that can set you apart.

Chapter 7

Making Choices for Success

Although it may be difficult to learn, wise decision-making will help you succeed in the future. You have already learned the process for making good decisions. As you go through that process, there are a few more things you should remember:

- Listen to others. You can learn from others' past successes and failures.
- Listen to yourself. Following your conscience will help you to respect yourself and will make other people respect you, too.
- Don't fear mistakes. If you are wise, the mistakes you make now will guide you in the future.
- Be responsible. You will have to deal with all the consequences of your decisions–both good and bad.

James is concerned that he might be gay. His whole life he has been attracted to men, but he keeps this inside. His friends make nasty jokes about gay characters on TV and famous people who have come out as homosexuals. James says nothing. Now his parents have started trying to get him to date their friends' daughter, but James always makes excuses.

James wishes that he had someone to talk to about these feelings, but he is afraid that people will be mean and make fun of him. But if he really starts to look, he can find supportive places where he can ask questions. He might go to his library and look for books and articles on teenage sexuality. He might look in the phone book for a teen hotline and see if he could get a referral to an agency that helps teenagers talk about sexual orientation. James might talk with an adult whom he trusts just so that he wouldn't have to keep all his feelings inside. These steps might help James sort through his mixed emotions.

When faced with a difficult decision, sometimes it may seem as though none of your choices looks very appealing. When this happens, you need to search for possibilities that you may not have seen earlier. Be creative. Sometimes it is hard to see beyond the most obvious choices, but a closer look can reveal options that you have not considered.

Other times, you may feel as though all your options seem attractive. This also can be overwhelming and confusing. How can you choose?

Tamecka was accepted into her three top choices of colleges, and she is having a very hard time deciding where to go. Hollister College is a small liberal-arts school, the State University of Springfield is large and public, and the Woudenberg University is private and prestigious. All have strong departments in business and economics, which is what she plans to study. The state university is less expensive, but the other two have offered her good scholarships. After visiting the schools, talking to professors and students, and writing a list of pros and cons for each institution, Tamecka decides to go with her gut feeling. She chooses the state university, because the African-American community there is strongest. Tamecka thinks it would be the best place for her to thrive.

Decision-making can seem dangerous and overwhelming. And it is, if you don't know how to approach it rationally. Once you have learned good decision-making skills, however, life becomes a lot easier to handle. You can confidently make your decisions, knowing that you have done everything that you can to ensure your success.

As you grow older, you will have more and more opportunities and therefore more decisions to make. With each one, you are learning more. Each good decision will help to improve your judgment, and each poor choice will help you to learn from experience.

If you remember the steps for smart decision-making, there is no problem too big for you. One of the best ways to succeed is by learning to decide well. Each decision you make leads you down the path to success.

Glossary

accomplish To achieve or make happen.

advice Opinion; guidance.

aggressive Forceful, pursuing what one wants with little regard for anything or anyone else.

assertive Positive, confident, self-assured, respectful.

conscience Inner awareness or voice telling you that something is right or wrong.

consequence Result; the effect of an action.

conviction Determination.

dominate To control one or more individuals or a situation.

immoral With selfish or evil intention or purpose.

manipulate To control or manage with hidden motives.

moral Honest, upright character or behavior.

opinion One's own thoughts, advice, or point of view.

option Choice.

passive Not speaking up or taking action.

passive-aggressive Going after objectives by lack of words or action; manipulating by silence or inactivity.

peer pressure Influence from people your own age to be like them.

perspective Judgment of a person or situation from a certain point of view; an overall view.

rationalize To explain with false or exaggerated reasons in order to convince someone else or yourself.

Where to Go for Help

Alcoholics Anonymous (AA)
P.O. Box 459
Grand Central Station
New York, NY 10163
(212) 870-3400
Web site: http://www.aa.org

Boys & Girls Clubs of America
1230 West Peachtree Street
    NW
Atlanta, GA 30309
(404) 815-5700
Web site: http://www.bgca.org

"Just Say No" International
2000 Franklin Street, Suite 400
Oakland, CA 94612
(800) 258-2766
(510) 451-6666
Web site:
http://www.justsayno.org

Narcotics Anonymous (NA)
World Service Office
19737 Nordhoff Place
Chatsworth, CA 91311
(818) 773-9999
e-mail: wso@aol.com

National Families in Action
2296 Henderson Mill Road,
    Suite 300
Atlanta, GA 30345-7239
(770) 934-6364
Web site:
http://www.emory. edu/NFIA/

Students Against Destructive
    Decisions (SADD)
P.O. Box 800
Marlboro, MA 10752
(508) 481-3568
Web site:
http://www.nat-sadd.org

In Canada
Addictions Foundation of
    Manitoba
1041 Portage Avenue
Winnipeg, MB R3G 0R8
(204) 944-6200

Alcoholics Anonymous (AA)
#202 Intergroup Office
234 Ellington Avenue E
Toronto, ON M4P 1K5
(416) 487-5591
Web site: http://www.aa.org

61

For Further Reading

Arnold, John D. *The Complete Problem Solver.* New York: Wiley, 1992.

Feller, Robyn M. *Everything You Need to Know About Peer Pressure.* New York: Rosen Publishing Group, 1997.

Kellogg, Mary Alice. *Hard Choices, Easy Decisions.* New York: Fireside Books, 1991.

McFarland, Rhoda. *Coping Through Assertiveness.* New York: Rosen Publishing Group, 1992.

Milios, Rita. *Discovering How to Make Good Choices.* New York: Rosen Publishing Group, 1992.

Smith, Sandra Lee. *Coping with Decision-Making.* New York: Rosen Publishing Group, 1993.

Index

A

abortion, 42
advice
    good or bad, 10–11, 20–24
    where to seek, 25–28
aggressive approach, 15, 16, 19
AIDS (acquired immunodeficiency
      syndrome), 22
arguments, pro and con, listing,
      42–44
assertive approach, 18–19
authorities, seeking advice from, 28

B

behavior
    aggressive, 15–16
    assertive, 18–19
    moral or immoral, 42, 45
    passive, 13–15, 19
    passive-aggressive, 16–18
blame, shifting, 52
body, listening to, 35–36
books, advice from, 27–28

C

cheating, 14, 44–47
clergy, advice from, 28
conscience, listening to, 35
consequences
    suffering, 54–55
    thinking through, 7, 45–46

D

decisions
    hurtful, 44–45
    making, 7–8, 10–11
domination, seeking, 23
drugs, 34–35
drunk driving, 53–54

E

emotions, 7, 33, 35

F

family, advice from, 27
feelings, listening to, 33
friends, choosing wisely, 25–26

G
goal, identifying, 37–38
guidance counselors, advice from, 27

H
homosexuality, 56–57

I
information
   gathering, 40–42
   withholding, 24

L
listening, importance of, 20–28

M
manipulation, 16
mistakes
   admitting, 54
   assessing importance of, 49, 51
   confronting, 48–49
   learning from, 56, 58
   serious, 52–55

O
options
   exploring, 7, 38–40, 57

P
passive-aggressive approach, 16, 18,
      19
passive approach, 13–14, 19

peer pressure, 26
peers, advice from, 25–26
Planned Parenthood, 41–42
pregnancy, 40–43

R
rationalization, 24–25, 45
reactions, physical, 34
responsibility, taking, 13–19, 56

S
sex, deciding on, 21–23
sexually transmitted disease
      (STD), 22
skill, decision-making, 7–8, 10–11,
      58
social workers, advice from, 28
success, choosing for, 56–58

T
teacher, advice from, 27
therapists, advice from, 28
time to consider, taking, 15, 46–47

V
voices, inner, 31–33

About the Author

Julie Parker is an ordained minister in the United Methodist Church with professional experience in counseling. She has written numerous books and articles for teenagers.

Photo Credits

Cover by Michael Brandt; p. 6 by Katherine Hsu; p. 50 by Maria Moreno; all other photos by Kim Sonsky.